"JUST KILL YOURSELF!"

"Just Kill Yourself!"

and Other Ways NOT to Navigate Conversations About Suicide

BRIANNA VALENTINE

Brianna Valentine

To my family members who have supported me,
to my friends who have brought me joy,
and to my therapist who has helped me process,

I thank you for your encouragement through my darkest times.
This relaunch wouldn't be possible without you all.

Thank you for believing in me.
Thank you for believing in this book.

PREFACE

Dear Reader,

I doubt myself preemptively because I already know that doubt from others is bound to come. I'm very discouraged. Can I write this book? Should I write this book? Will people care? Will people trust me? Will I cause more harm than good? Is this a stupid idea? I've many fears about this book. They are all valid, as all feelings are, but I still worry that they may be coming from the wrong place.

It's important to me that I don't discuss the serious and fragile topic of suicide recklessly. I realize the potential influence that I may have, and it's a frighteningly huge responsibility. That being said, it's imperative that anyone reading this knows three things about this book:

First and foremost, this book is written from my point of view, as someone who has struggled with suicidal thoughts for almost a decade and never received the care that I so desperately needed. I'm not a medical or mental health care professional, as I will mention frequently throughout the book. I am an expert on only my own experience. Despite this, I've made hundreds of friends and acquaintances over the years who also struggle with suicidal thoughts, and it has enlightened me to the similar experiences of others. I have formed and analyzed this information using a lot more than just my own feelings. Even so, I am not an expert in all things suicide related. Take what I say seriously, but please also weigh it against other information.

Secondly, no one should open this book expecting to find a cure-all for suicidal ideation. Everyone who struggles with suicidal thoughts is an individual with their own unique experiences. The goal of this book is to facilitate a conversation with you, the reader, and to offer you tips on how to navigate future conversations about suicide. This book was written with the hopes that people in support roles as well as those who struggle with suicidal thoughts could be helped. My hope is that this book will open your eyes to some things you may have never considered before. At the very least, I hope it gives you some insight about a difficult question: what happens to the people that don't die, but don't get better? This book is not meant to put people down for not knowing how to navigate these conversations. It takes time and practice to get better at this. If I used our conversation as an example in this book, know that I hold no resentment toward you. There is no reason for me to have expected others to know how to handle these conversations before now. Thank you for being a perfect example of what not to do.

Lastly, this book is a lot to digest all at once, so please do not overwhelm yourself. Check in as necessary and take breaks when you need to.

This book needed to be written. I needed to write this book, and I needed to write it in a way that felt honest and helpful to the little version of me that navigated these things alone for over a decade. I needed to give hope to others who feel the same way. And part of me wrote this book to insist to the general population that people who are suicidal are still competent.

It's time to clear some space for the ones who want to get better on their own terms, so make way! Here I, and hundreds of thousands of silenced voices, come.

Thank you, and please enjoy.

- Brianna Valentine

INTRODUCTION

The first time I attempted suicide, I was eleven years old. I remember contemplating the action as I lay face first on the carpet in an empty room of my house. It was a sunny Saturday morning. I don't recall feeling sad, just defeated. I was struggling to adjust to a new house after being evicted and losing all of my things, grappling with the first warning signs of my parents' divorce, and succumbing to the idea that feeling like an outcast and being tormented in school would never end. I realized that these issues were uncontrollable. There was nothing that I could do to make any of it better. Understanding that these issues would never go away, it proved to be too much for me. I wrote a heartfelt note explaining the ways that these things in my life were hurting me, and I concluded with a line saying, "I just don't want to do this anymore."

I got up from the floor and walked to the bathroom, thinking about a conversation I had with my mom about how taking too much medicine could kill you. I grabbed the Children's Claritin chewables from the bathroom cabinet and, knowing that my normal dosage was one, took two, certain that death awaited me in the near future. Unfortunately for eleven year old me, those two chewable tablets didn't give me so much as a stomach ache, and I went on to endure every stressor that I had outlined in my suicide note and more.

Kids doing dumb things and lacking an understanding of the way things work is funny, and that story makes me (and others) laugh when I tell it. However, it marked a very important day in my life. That day was the first time that I acknowledged that I wanted to die. I came to full terms with the idea that I wouldn't be here anymore and took action to make that happen, no matter how stupid and ineffective I now know that action was. It was the first time of many that the nagging urge to give up finally silenced the voices of comfort.

I grew up during the closing cusp of the largely accepted "we don't believe in mental illness" mindset from parents and their children, alike, so getting help was a battle in and of itself. This mindset came from the stigma surrounding mental illness. The stigma could have been caused by any combination of lack of education, unfair representation in the media, and the poor treatment of mental illnesses throughout history. In recent years, we've been more supportive of those who suffer from mental illness, due to improvement in each of these areas.

It's been a decade since I first started violently struggling with the ideas of pushing through or giving up. For a while, I would have long periods of being okay. Even when things were bad, I'd have no problem making it to tomorrow, and only every once in a while would I have a really tough day. When that would happen, as long as I could make it to bed that night and wake up the next day, I would be fine.

By the time I reached high school, my desire to give up was equally as powerful as my conditioning to keep going. At age fourteen, I'm not sure that I had any specific reason to keep going. It's just what was expected. People tell you that you're not allowed to give up, that better days lie ahead, and when you're that young, you don't know any better. You trust them and you keep going. I have a vivid memory from this time of walking into my father's office in our home.

"Father," I said, on the verge of tears. "I've been getting bullied a lot in school, and I think it's really affecting me. I feel like I can't focus on anything, and I really think I need help."

"Hmm," my father began. Without looking up from his computer, he said, "You'll be aight," and sent me on my way.

By the time high school was ending, most of that conditioning I just mentioned had been re-conditioned out of me. I faced so much mental and emotional abuse from people I thought were my friends, from some teachers, and from miscellaneous students at my school, that I had almost lost all hope of things ever getting better. I thought that it was all my fault. If it had been possible for me to feel worse at that point, the thought that I was the one responsible for my pain would have done it. Every Instagram post about mental health told me that the reason I wasn't getting better was because *I* hadn't tried hard enough or reached out. So I tried one last time.

"Mom," I started, sitting on the edge of her bed. "I think I might be depressed. It's something that I've known for a long time, but I think a diagnosis would be helpful and would lead me towards the help I need."

"Well, I think that you just want to abuse pills like your father..." is all I heard before I walked out of the room. The blatant lack of concern from both of my parents now was devastating.

I'm sure my parents would say that they had no clue about the gravity of the pain that I was experiencing, and that they had even less of a clue about how to help me with it, given that we did not have health insurance or enough money to send me to therapy or buy any medication that I may have subsequently been prescribed. Maybe they even thought that it might just blow over at some point. Alas, here I am, twenty-one years old and too tired to battle my common sense any longer. I keep telling myself, "It's okay. I know I haven't had a good day in several months, but tomorrow is a new one! It gets better," but it's getting old, and I feel stupid.

For a while, religion was my only saving grace, no pun intended. It was all I had to hold on to. I gave everything to the god I prayed to in hopes that my pain wasn't meaningless, and that something better was coming for me. When my prayers became more frequent and the answers became less so, I lost my faith. I started to realize just how much pain I was covering up with "God has a plan for me." The COVID-19 pandemic arriving before I could finish my second year of college took my struggles to a new level.

If Instagram is good for anything, it showed me that the pandemic taught a lot of people what it's like when they no longer have distractions from their suicidal thoughts, and I was no exception. My whole life was thrown off course and the state of the world brought back every feeling of worthlessness, confusion, and purposelessness that I was repressing with my vigorous class schedule.

I tried going to therapy, but it became clear very quickly that the therapist and I weren't a good match. This was on top of the fact that the insurance I was using was through the school I could no longer attend (due to the pandemic), so I only had about two months to get my therapy "done" before I could no longer pay for my sessions. It was around then that I realized I needed a new kind of help.

Anyone who has dealt with severe, unattended-to suicidal thoughts (especially for an extended period of time) can recognize that the general population's views of and approaches to conversations about suicide are lackluster at best. This stems from three main things:

1. Suicidal people are misunderstood on the most basic level.

For there to be a chance that suicidal people can be encouraged to live, there needs to be an effort to understand what they are struggling with. Without understanding, there is no connection between Someone Learning to Navigate (hereon abbreviated as SLN) and the experience of people who struggle with suicidal thoughts. Without that connection, SLN has no incentive to make any change to their behavior for their own sake or someone else's.

2. Most people don't know how to navigate conversations surrounding suicide properly.

Remedying this requires work from SLN in addition to conversations with Someone Who Is Suicidal (hereon abbreviated as SWIS) to figure out the best approach to this.

3. Every suicidal person is a unique individual.

Everyone's suicidal thoughts are unique, not only in the way they feel to each person who experiences them, but also in where they come from, the work it will take to heal from them, and the awareness that SWIS has in regard to them.

I am an expert on my own experience, but I cannot give a foolproof guide on how to talk anyone who is suicidal. I can, however, offer tangible advice that can be applied to most conversations with SWIS. This soon-to-come advice will hopefully spark discussions that lead to solutions that feel good for everyone. First, here is some context.

Overview

In general, the perspectives about suicide that we hear most often are from psychiatrists, grieving loved ones, and regretful/recovered survivors. While their perspectives are equally important and deserve to be heard, we need more than just their testimonies to move forward in this conversation. Hearing from only these three groups often leaves the people currently struggling with suicidal thoughts feeling unseen and misunderstood. Overlooking the perspective of those who are *actively* suicidal has created a lack of sufficient understanding about what is most helpful to SWIS. The conversation is dominated by "experts" who feel confident enough to speak over suicidal people, when SWIS should be leading the conversation. Being in situations where I am spoken over and where someone claims to be speaking for my best interests, while really just spreading ideas that are harmful to me, has made my journey toward healing much harder. I have always felt that I wouldn't be listened to if I sought help.

Not having someone who was actively suicidal in the public eye —to discuss the reality of what recovery looks like for SWIS, how not every tool that is suggested will be effective for everyone, and how SWIS can cope until afforded professional help—negatively affected the way that people navigated conversations about suicide with me. Until these things are included in conversations about suicide on a large scale, we can't have the conversations necessary to help suicidal people take the first steps toward their healing.

I'm in a unique position writing this book because I still experience suicidal thoughts. Ironically, that tragic fact offers me a few wonderful advantages in the context of the information I wish to share.

I cannot separate myself from the issue, since the success of this book's instruction is instrumental to my own chances of getting better, but that incentivizes me to ensure that the information provided here is genuine. Not only will I be harmed if I fail to effectively represent those who struggle similarly, but I could reinforce the social stigma surrounding suicide and potentially set the conversation back decades.

Despite this incentive to advise as best I can, my inability to remove myself from the subject matter also means that some readers will be less inclined to take me seriously. Returning to the social stigma surrounding suicide, some readers may not want to approach this book with an open mind and an intent to learn. *Why should we listen to her? She's obviously not well, mentally.* As correct as that sentiment about the state of my mind may be, I still have valuable insight into the world of SWIS that SLN may never otherwise be able to understand. I'm certain that at least a few people will try to spin this book into something it's not, claiming that it's angst-y, a cry for attention, or a plea for pity. If you are the person that opened this book in search of something to be angry about, I encourage you to give it a chance. This very well could spark a new understanding that will change the lives of suicidal people for generations.

My goal is to introduce information about the lived experiences of SWIS that is not well known, or even completely unspoken about. I will then explore the ways in which conversations about suicide are currently navigated, and how to navigate them in a way that is less harmful (and more helpful) to SWIS.

PART ONE

FACTORS THAT SHAPE OUR CONVERSATIONS ABOUT SUICIDE

Dispelling Myths and Misinformation

In order for this book to be an effective tool, you, as SLN, need to rid your mind of everything you've ever been told about suicide. While it's unlikely that *every* bit of that information is wrong, it's still important to start with a clear head so that this new information can reach you. As I mentioned before, the stigma surrounding suicide is something that has prevented me from getting help for years. When I've tried to have conversations about my struggles, the stigma surrounding the topic has often steered people in the wrong direction. I believe that more understanding is the first step in overcoming this.

Stigma

In my experience, the stigma surrounding suicide is heavily perpetuated by some people's refusal to take SWIS seriously. I can remember many times when my parents or teachers dismissed my concerns, insisting that I was only bringing up my suicidal thoughts as an excuse to get out of work or school. I have also had experiences with people who insist that SWIS only claims to be suicidal for attention, or people who won't take SWIS seriously because they have preconceived ideas about what it really means to be suicidal.

Some people learning to navigate believe that SWIS struggles with suicidal thoughts because "they just can't see the good in life". People have full blown arguments with me about this topic because they are so attached to the idea that being suicidal is synonymous with being cynical. They insist that my being suicidal causes me to see bad in the world that isn't there. For me, this is the furthest thing from the truth.

When I'm not in the middle of a suicidal crisis, I experience a lot of good things. Even during a crisis, I have the ability to laugh and smile. But crisis or no crisis, I refuse to shut out all of my feelings that aren't inherently positive to convince myself that I am happy when I am not. Therefore, when I am entering a crisis, it is easy for the people around me to perceive my struggles as "negativity." I will always choose to be honest with myself about my feelings, my level of comfort, and my level of enjoyment. This is not because of my suicidal thoughts, but because I respect myself enough to take care of myself mentally and emotionally. My willingness to be honest with myself about the fact that I'm not doing well is not a symptom of being suicidal; it's a sign that I'm on my way to healing.

"Toxic Positivity"

I've noticed that there's been a huge wave of what has been labeled as "toxic positivity" on the internet. While I never had a term to describe it until recently, I have vocalized my seething hatred for this for a while. Toxic positivity is very easy to spot if you know how to look for it. Anyone that has an incessant need to shut down any sign of negative emotions is toxically positive. Think of someone saying "C'mon we only allow positive vibes here. Think of the bright side," when someone expresses feelings of grief after their grandfather died. I think the "toxic positivity crew" is the biggest enemy when it comes to fighting the stigma that specifically stems from this idea that suicidal people "can't see the good in life."

I, SWIS, see a lot of good in life. I have many wonderful things for myself. I have been very lucky in many regards, and I am able to recognize that. However, my struggles with suicide are so much more complex than me being self-aware enough to acknowledge the things in life that have been severely unpleasant. Me entering a crisis is something much deeper than feeling sad about an event in my life or feeling lonely and as if nobody loves me. When trying to navigate any conversation about an unpleasant experience, and especially one about suicide, it's important to remember that every expression of negative feeling does not need to be followed by advice to "make the most" out of something that someone else is really struggling with. This is especially true when it comes to situations that are objectively negative (e.g. the passing of someone that this person really cared about, a terminal diagnosis, financial struggles). It's obnoxious to ask that of someone in pain. Furthermore, it isn't good advice. Creating a false reality of peace and positivity to cope with struggles can be really hurtful to your trust in yourself.

I used to be the toxically positive person that I'm haranguing about now, and it damaged my ability to be honest with myself for years. I can assure you, as much as I insisted to myself and everyone who tolerated me that there was good in everything and everyone, it didn't stop me from being suicidal. Instead of acknowledging the negative feelings I was experiencing, I'd beat myself up for thinking about it, and I'd try to recondition my brain to float in a pool of positivity at all times. This, of course, didn't work. I couldn't stop myself from experiencing negativity, nor could I prevent myself from feeling sad. I was unkind to myself for experiencing normal human emotions and then projected the negativity I was bottling up onto other people in their times of need. Being toxically positive made it harder for me to take care of myself mentally and emotionally.

I spent all of my time convincing myself that the negativity I felt was unwarranted and shameful. It made it hard for people to want to be around me, because anyone else experiencing negative feelings threatened to shatter my illusion of an unwaveringly positive world that I'd created for myself. I knew that this illusion being broken could've sent me spiraling in a way that I might never have recovered from, so I fought their feelings in a manner that really damaged them.

SLN may think that trying to prevent SWIS from acknowledging their negative emotions is effective in preventing SWIS from entering a crisis. As much as their heart may be in the right place, shaming SWIS for speaking up about pain that they are feeling, the way that it is affecting them, and/or the fact that they need help will only be detrimental to SWIS. When you try to silence SWIS's cries for help with the positivity that you scavenge for in their pain, you create an environment where they feel that they are welcome, but only conditionally. They will only be tolerated when they are doing well. These environments don't feel safe for SWIS. Yes, I'm very vocal about the terrible things that I feel, but being suicidal doesn't magically create negativity in my life. Being suicidal *does* make it harder for me to process the negative things that come my way. What might be a miniscule inconvenience to SLN can send me spiraling into a battle with suicide that I'll nearly lose. This misunderstanding has been weaponized against me since I first opened up about my suicidal thoughts.

Condescension and Disbelief

SLN may also choose to dismiss SWIS because of the widely spread and false belief that suicidal people "don't actually want to die." People have insisted to me that SWIS wanting to escape their pain by dying is (somehow) different than wanting to die. This insistence is dismissive of SWIS struggles, and this ultimately can be dangerous. Aside from that, for SLN to say this, it means that they are either:

> A. consciously or unconsciously condescendingly thinking about SWIS's battle with suicide as not real

or

> B. making an effort to comfort themselves.

If SWIS opens up to you about the pain they're experiencing, you should never decide for yourself that the feelings they've directly expressed to you are not accurate or disingenuous. In doing so, you'd be choosing to ignore their cries for help and disregarding the courage it takes for SWIS to reach out to somebody for help. It is absolutely true that some people who made suicide attempts in the past have expressed that they never actually wanted to die. However, it is important that you allow SWIS to express that to you themselves, if that is the case. Just assuming can be very harmful to someone, whether or not they later agree with you. Saying that suicidal people "don't actually want to die" is only comforting to the person who is not suicidal. It provides them a degree of separation from how serious the issue is while depriving the suicidal person of the understanding they need to get better. By insisting that the desire to end their pain with death is somehow different from "actually" wanting to die, SLN feels that they are better equipped to handle the situation—or even to fix it entirely. Once you've decided that this person actually wants to live and is just feeling a little down, you can send them Instagram quotes about pushing through and remembering how loved they are, and the problem will fix itself... right?

As complex of a concept as suicide and suicidal ideation is, the meaning of the term is not opaque. Composed of Latin roots, "sui" means "of oneself" and "cide" means "to kill." I am suicidal. I want to die. I do often think about how suicide would end my pain. I also am often tossed into a battle with my suicidal thoughts when faced with my pain. That doesn't change the fact that, when struggling with these thoughts, my end goal is death, and it certainly does not mean that I "don't want to die."

Missing Perspectives

Suicidal people are not allowed to engage in conversations about suicide enough. In most media that we're exposed to on a large scale, we hear from three main perspectives: psychiatrists/therapists, grieving loved ones, and the recovered survivors of suicidal thoughts and ideation. All of these perspectives are important and deserve to be heard, as they all offer their own unique set of information, but centering SWIS's voice would offer us perspectives on this topic that could teach us a more effective way to encourage people to live.

Most therapists and psychiatrists function as wonderful support systems for their patients. They help them understand the chemical side of what they're struggling with and offer them tools that are crucial in the healing process. I insist that the ultimate goal in having conversations about suicide with SWIS is to help them feel supported enough to eventually get professional help. However, the professionals can only ever help their patients and clients with what that patient or client is able to share with the professional. Something is clearly missing from this conversation. If professionals only ever get to work with the individuals who make it to therapy, they can't effectively speak on some aspects of the struggles of those who they never get to help. In terms of emotion, unless the therapist or the psychiatrist dealt with their own untreated suicidal thoughts for an extended time before becoming a professional, they can only know as much as their patients are able to convey. This can leave out chunks of important information when it comes to the professional knowing what danger signs to look out for in their patients, and also when it comes to the professional then furthering knowledge and awareness about suicidal ideation, what it feels like for SWIS, and how to navigate it. Professionals are wonderful at analyzing data, using that knowledge to give people tools to help them feel better, and at writing informational pieces so that other people can have an idea of what suicidal people are going through. For this reason, the voice of professionals is absolutely vital in this conversation, and it is imperative that we never silence the professionals who have helped us propel this conversation this far. But we need to add the voice of SWIS into this conversation because without it, we are missing a huge piece of the puzzle and will be prevented from moving the conversation any further forward. Information directly from the primary source (i.e SWIS) is always good to have. By the time research done by professionals about suicide and suicidal people reaches the public, it has been heavily filtered in order for the professional to relay the information that they believe is important in a concise manner. Hearing SWIS's thoughts directly from them allows that middleman to be cut out. When SWIS speaks for themselves, you can hear, analyze, and interpret for yourself the information they're trying to convey. It also allows people to speak more freely about what they're struggling with without the fear of being placed on a psychiatric hold. The overwhelming fear of involuntary hospitalization prevents many suicidal people from being completely honest and open when asking for help. Allowing SWIS their own platform to speak about their struggles ultimately allows for more effective conversations about how to move forward with help and treatment, even if those conversations are more intense and uncomfortable.

For the very short time that I was able to do therapy, I attended because I was having a harder time dealing with suicidal thoughts on my own than ever before. But when it came time to actually start unpacking things in therapy, I didn't feel safe enough to even hint at anything to do with mood dysregulation, let alone the unbearable suicidal thoughts I was struggling with. I know several other people who attended therapy to get help with their suicidal thoughts, and to this day, have not been able to effectively have a conversation about it with a professional due to a fear of being hospitalized. I know that a lot of therapists insist that institutionalization and reporting to the police is the very last resort for them. As much as that might be true, the patient's fear that it could happen at all, combined with the fact that they have no clue where that line lies, is enough to scare some people out of talking about the things that made them decide to start therapy in the first place.

Personally, a big part of my ongoing struggle with suicidal thoughts is that no one has known how to navigate my struggles in a way that doesn't make me feel gawked at, "other than", dramatic, or erratic. I've found that I need to be able to talk about my suicidal thoughts with the same bluntness with which they enter my mind: "Lately, I've wanted to kill myself every second of every day, and now I feel like I don't have a reason not to." I need a professional that I can't traumatize with my matter-of-fact attitude toward my suicidal thoughts. And I need my suicidal thoughts to be assessed with the same attitude a doctor would assess a gash on someone's arm: "This is serious. Alright. Let's figure it out."

Some people definitely need a much gentler approach to their feelings, especially if they've been dealing with them for a much shorter period of time. However, that's why it's important that we have these conversations and give people the option, the space, and the support to heal on their own terms and in ways that will help them long term. It's vital that we discuss how intense suicidal thoughts can be and not have our immediate reaction be to send someone straight to the hospital without passing go or collecting $200. The professionals have done and continue to do amazing work, but we still need to open up some space for the people who are actively struggling to offer deeper insight into how we can help people.

As SWIS, I very often am spoken to by grieving loved ones and acquaintances of people who died by suicide. Most often, they share with me the pain that their loved one's suicide caused them and the fact that they had no clue that it was coming. Talking about how they feel, how they're coping, and what they need can help other loved ones of SWIS feel supported and understood—and it is essential that we uplift the voices of these people. They offer a wonderful contribution to the conversation about suicide. However, it doesn't offer any information about how to help SWIS, or what steps to take when you learn that someone is suicidal. Allowing SWIS to be the center of this conversation would add another perspective and more insight into what SWIS is going through.

You'll hear people talk about how if someone is "saying their final goodbyes," discussing doing things "for the last time,", or suddenly seeming like everything is fine, it's a telltale sign of someone who is about to attempt suicide. This might be a good rule of thumb for some people, but it doesn't apply to everyone. It's important that we discuss how we can help the people who spend more time alone and aren't around anyone to showcase these signs, the people who know that doing certain things will alert others to what they're planning, and the people who know that saying *anything* about suicide is considered taboo. We need to discuss how to help the people who are convinced that even thinking about suicide is the most awful thing one can do, and because of that, are more inclined to go through with it. All of these insights can be best provided by the people who actively struggle with suicidal thoughts, as we are most familiar with what has helped us in the past and how that evolves with time. We know best what sentiments are helpful vs. harmful, how to repair damage done by a conversation that was navigated improperly, and what the next step is when a solution doesn't work as intended. Being trapped in this society where suicide is a taboo subject and something that shan't be heard, seen, or spoken about is really harmful to SWIS, especially when it comes to reaching out for help. Always feeling shut down after sharing my struggles with my friends and family has been most of my experience. In looking for support, I was almost always offered shame. This made it harder for me to reach out in the future and *continues* to prolong my journey to healing. Sadly, this is all too common, and too many people never reach out for help because they are embarrassed, they feel that their family would be no help, they've been taught that they should handle their struggles silently and alone, or they fear that no one will take them seriously.

In many cases, families don't get talked to about what is or was going on with SWIS. Between strict religious views, the idea that suicide and conversations about it are taboo, and the embarrassment that comes with struggling with suicidal thoughts, there is seldom an environment where SWIS feels safe enough to speak freely. Allowing SWIS to speak openly about their struggles in the public eye creates a starting point that would assuage some tension, misinformation, and fear surrounding this topic, and it would open up further opportunities for a life-saving dialogue between SWIS and a loved one.

Loved ones (being the usual first instinct of who to talk to when you're struggling with anything, especially something as serious as suicide) will sometimes get put on the spot with issues like this. Because we don't talk about these issues enough, people don't know how to navigate these conversations when they occur. Often, people's first instinct in these conversations is to shut down the idea of suicide. It comes from a good place, but it leaves no room for a deeper conversation. Remedying the symptom (i.e. the desire to die by suicide) can only be temporary if the underlying cause is never addressed. It's important that SWIS gets to talk about the ways to address these underlying causes with their loved ones and find more effective solutions in the long run.

Representation in the Media

I used to look up to a lot of the survivors in the media (mostly music artists and actors) that talked about their previous struggles with suicidal thoughts. Between the fear surrounding opening up about the topic and the people that have always tried to silence the voices that do speak up, there aren't many survivors in the media. The ones that I did see held a special place in my heart, and I felt very grateful for their bravery. But the longer that my struggles went on, the harder I found it to relate to what some of those people were saying. Most survivors in the media focus on what their life is like now that they're recovered and how wonderful it feels to no longer struggle with suicidal thoughts. Oftentimes, they offer a story about the lowest point in their struggle with suicide and talk about the fact that their life is better now than it was then. They typically conclude by talking about how they couldn't have had this amazing life if they had died by suicide. In the media, the main focus is insisting that recovery is possible.

When I first began to realize that I was struggling with my mental well-being, hearing this perspective was so important to me. At that point in my journey with suicidal thoughts, I didn't know anything about what was happening in my mind. I didn't know that I wasn't the only person in the world who felt this way, I wasn't aware that therapy was something that could help me if I wasn't experiencing auditory hallucinations and paranoia, and I had no clue that there were people who made it out on the other side to recovery. These public figures who spoke out about this helped me—and likely many others—to feel less alone. They helped me get a grasp on the next steps that I wanted to take in my journey to healing. For this reason, we need to make sure that these people will always be given the space to talk about their experience.

As I got a better grasp on my struggles and began trying several different approaches to healing, I became keenly aware that a combination of my family's poverty and lack of belief in mental health made it so that therapy was the necessary step that I couldn't take. Around this time, those same figures in the media suddenly ceased to feel helpful to me. Conversations that are recovery-focused are not helpful for people like me, who didn't have the access to the necessary tools for healing. There's a point where the problem is no longer whether or not they know that healing is possible and what steps to take to heal, but that the steps they need to take are not accessible for them. Admittedly, it became frustrating for me, as a child trying to navigate her suicidal thoughts all on her own, that these conversations hadn't evolved. I felt like I was a few steps ahead of any advice that anyone had for me.

For people like me, who feel that their struggles and experiences with suicidal thoughts go beyond what is represented by the people in the media, we need to add the voice of SWIS to cover a larger range of experience and a different, more inclusive view of what battling suicide looks like. Since most of what we are currently exposed to are conversations that are recovery-focused, we hear a lot of stories about survivors who experience regret. These conversations in particular have been especially harmful to the way that SLN chooses to navigate a conversation about suicide with me. Since the media is responsible for most of what people believe about suicide in general, many people in my life who are learning to navigate have held onto the repeated narrative about regret. Based on the information they received, they believed that I also experience feelings of regret, or that regret is something that will soon come to me. In holding onto this idea, these people also dismissed my struggles as something trivial that will pass with time.

It is my experience that SLN is missing variation in their knowledge about people who currently struggle (and who have struggled in the past) with suicidal thoughts. Only hearing the perspective of recovered survivors who express their regret means that the people learning to navigate don't get adequate information about how painful struggling with suicidal thoughts can be, how seriously the struggles need to be taken, how long it takes to recover from them, and how much support is required for SWIS to get to a point in recovery where they can feel or express regret. This lack of variation in what is shown in the media has caused people in my life to laugh away my cries for help, viewing them as nothing more than "a phase." Experiencing this repeatedly has been extremely demoralizing.

As SWIS, there have been countless times where people wanted to make me feel stupid for experiencing suicidal thoughts. I've had my share of ups and downs with my struggles, and there have been times where I was certain that I had managed to find a permanent solution. It would feel really good to tell the people I love how well I was doing, especially those who knew how much I struggled on a regular basis. When I would tell the people I loved that I was feeling better, some were too eager to say, "I told you so," and ask me how stupid I felt for ever wanting to die.

Obviously, as of writing this, I am far from recovery. When I hit a low after telling everyone how well I had been doing, it is so much harder to open up than before. Struggling with suicidal thoughts is already something that feels so shameful for the person struggling, even though it shouldn't. In those times of need, I was more worried about letting people down—now knowing their true feelings about my struggles—than I was about reaching out for help. Their reactions always stemmed from their inherent belief that my struggles were temporary and were never something that needed to be tended to. This goes back to the media only ever promoting conversations about recovery.

People in my life who are learning to navigate frequently draw comparisons between me and the recovered survivors in the media. These people often lose sight of the privileges those survivors were afforded in their journey. Be it therapy, a supportive family and friends, or things as simple as being able to take time to recover. These are all things that not everyone is lucky enough to have. With therapy being painfully expensive, some people having work schedules that barely leave enough time for sleep—let alone time to focus on healing—and the fact that so many are in the hands of people who don't believe that someone's mind can be unhealthy, this comparison can be very discouraging. For me, the point of the comparison is always either to tell me that I should try harder to be like those survivors or that I must be lying about what I'm struggling with because my experience doesn't align with what they've seen in the media (which is often their only other exposure to people who struggle with suicidal thoughts).

Furthermore, after listening to recovery-focused conversations, I frequently found myself thinking things like: "I must be different.

My suicidal thoughts must be *really* bad. This recovered person didn't mention anything about the thoughts I'm thinking or the feelings I'm feeling. They just said that they got better. I'm not getting any better. They said it happened when they were fifteen. I'm eighteen, and I'm not better. It must really be over for me." This proved to be very dangerous for me, especially early on in my journey through my struggles with suicide. By allowing more voices of people who *actively* struggle with suicidal thoughts, there would be a better awareness of what the process of recovery looks like.

Currently, I feel that I struggle to feel connected to the people in the media who lead regret-focused conversations about suicide. When someone is appointed as a voice for suicidal people and they begin to talk about regret, what they're actually doing is being a voice for people who have recovered. As someone who is actively struggling with suicidal thoughts, I can't relate to conversations about recovery. I don't feel heard or represented when someone is talking about regret or the relief that comes with being recovered. In actuality, I feel left out of a conversation that is quite literally life or death for me. Lacking this connection makes it harder for me to lead my own conversations about suicide because the people I talk to often think what they've heard in the media is representative of all (or even most) of the people in the world who struggle with suicidal thoughts. It is so important that we continue to allow space for those who are talking about ongoing recovery, as those who have recovered need just as much support as those who are currently struggling.

I need someone in the media who I feel connected to, not only so I don't feel alone, but also so that the people around me will have a better understanding of what I'm struggling with and help me create environments in which I am more likely to survive.

However, there still needs to be some balance in the topics of conversation. I also believe that SWIS would benefit from more people distinguishing between conversations about suicide and conversations about recovery. Conversations about suicide, in general, will help SLN to better understand what SWIS is experiencing when they're struggling heavily and how to best support them during that time. Conversations about recovery focus more on the hope that people can feel after being recovered, the struggles that remain after someone is recovered, and anything else that someone who is recovered feels will serve them.

The lack of separation of these topics has caused me harm that has taken almost a decade for me to put into words. I've been left with only frustration and isolation, and no way to convey to people exactly what was bothering me. Centering the voice of someone who discusses what it's like to be actively suicidal will offer more people who are suicidal someone to look up to. In turn, more people learning to navigate will have a better idea of what SWIS is struggling with. Those who struggle with suicidal thoughts will be able to experience hope for their recovery.

Having conversations about someone's accomplishments post-recovery is meant to be encouraging for SWIS, and in many cases, it is very helpful. On the other hand, highlighting the ways a survivor's life has changed without also offering an account of how hard recovery can be and how long it can take to be considered "recovered," can leave SWIS feeling anxious and confused. Having examples of the beauty of recovery, when missing conversation about the work it takes to recover, can make it harder for SWIS to feel that good days are coming. We need both voices to create balance in the media. If we have too many voices focusing only on recovery, we will lack realistic expectations for people who are currently struggling. If we have too many voices of people who are actively struggling, we will lack hope for a future of recovery. It's important that we hear these voices together to create the complete narrative: recovery is possible if SWIS wants to recover, has access to the tools necessary to do so, and is willing to pace themselves.

Keeping an Open Mind

It's important that society is open to learning new information about suicide and suicidal thoughts if we hope to erase the stigma that so often prevents people from getting help. Unfortunately, I've met too many people that refuse to open their minds to new information and educate themselves any further. It's not just the people who don't think suicide is a real problem, either. I know people who feel neutrally about suicide and who don't want to be seen as someone who doesn't care, but would rather keep the issue at an arm's length. Involving themselves any more would open them and their actions up to criticism. This behavior can look like someone engaging in surface-level conversations about suicide but refusing to educate themselves further. Many of these people fear that if they take the time to listen to new information, they'd learn that they are (or have been) a part of the problem. Especially with an issue as serious as suicide, that's a very scary road to go down. If they were to learn that they were acting in a way that is harmful, they would have to make a commitment to changing their behavior. It takes effort to have these conversations and change behaviors accordingly. For some, that's too much. It can also be painful to learn that you've harmed people unintentionally, especially if you decide that you'd like to apologize.

For others, educating themselves further would mean admitting that they are facing struggles of their own. It's hard for some people to cope with the fact that they are experiencing suicidal thoughts, especially when they come from a background that doesn't believe in mental illness. So many people I've met have a deep, troubled past with suicidal thoughts. In many cases, they didn't have access to professional help and support, and had to use other coping mechanisms—convincing themselves that their suicidal thoughts were a "phase," convincing themselves that they weren't actually suicidal, or convincing themselves that they needed to figure it out on their own. The families that they come from have a deep attachment to the toxic mentalities that they were raised with. For them, educating themselves about suicide would mean acknowledging for the first time that suicidal thoughts exist and are something that people really struggle with.

Many adults of the older generations are attached to the idea that mental illness is "new" and that people didn't struggle before Gen Z. They fail to realize the very simple fact that people have died by suicide for centuries. More recently, we're finding people who are brave enough to speak up about it. There are also people who are completely detached from the issue. They may not know (or are unaware of) anyone who is suicidal, and therefore believe that this couldn't happen to them and they don't need this information. They may feel contempt for suicidal people, think that their struggles come from a lack of intelligence or social awareness, or they may just believe that people struggling with suicidal thoughts shouldn't be anyone else's problem—suicidal people should be left to figure it out for themselves. And they may just not care. No matter which of these categories you fall into, if any, it's always beneficial to educate yourself. With an issue like suicide, you can never be too informed. Suicidal thoughts can haunt anyone, and deepening your well of knowledge surrounding this topic could save someone's life. If enough people agree to learn, so many people could be saved.

Support Systems: Helpful vs. Harmful

When we don't allow space for SWIS to be able to take care of themselves, they can be left feeling that their problems aren't as important as the things other people want from them (e.g. showing up to work, getting good grades, going to parties). This prevents the person who is suicidal from taking the necessary time to acknowledge their struggles and ask for help and support. It's important that we realize that this conversation can't be tabled for a later date. We lose people to suicide all too often, and the idea that suicidal people are expected to just "hold on" when they've got nothing to hold on to makes this problem worse. We need to be having real, painful conversations about this topic if we want to encourage people to live on a wider scale. This is not something that can be saved for later because there isn't a later for everybody.

There's an unfair expectation for suicidal people to push their issues aside for various reasons. Expecting SWIS to stash away their struggles can be dangerous, and it can prevent them from getting the help they need. Many unsupportive families, for example, will insist that SWIS should just stop talking about their issues. While it is completely understandable that trying to be the support system for someone who is suicidal can feel exhausting if you don't know how to navigate these conversations, the remedy is to become more practiced and to gain knowledge with the subject matter, not to try to disguise or ignore the issue. Too often loved ones will take a stance of "I don't want to hear about it." When SWIS is stopped from sharing their struggles, it might provide the person trying to support them with the false comfort of "they haven't been talking about it as much, they must be doing better." In reality, the suicidal person is now fighting an impossibly difficult battle all on their own, and they now feel less comfortable speaking up and asking for help, even when they know they're about to lose.

For others, there is the expectation for SWIS to stop experiencing their suicidal thoughts. "Stop being so negative!" This comes from a belief that the pain is not real or the idea that suicidal thoughts are equivalent to just having a bad day. These people don't realize that there is a mental battle involved when someone is suicidal, and they think the person who is suicidal isn't "trying hard enough." This makes SWIS feel hopeless, that their problems won't be seen as real, and that they should not bother reaching out for help. The concept that their problems are not "real" is an idea that SWIS will internalize and start to convince themselves of. SWIS may try to convince themselves that if they always push away their thoughts and struggles, those things will somehow fix themselves or go away. This belief is rooted in ignorance and shame—and it is dangerous.

"Suicide is never an option," may seem like a helpful thing to say to someone who is suicidal, but it rarely is. Most often, it ends up being really harmful. I hear this phrase a lot, whether it's other people saying it to SWIS or SWIS saying it to themselves. Suicidal people often say this to themselves in an attempt to soothe their pain, especially when they don't have access to the support they need to properly address their issues. People who aren't suicidal seem to use this phrase as a bat to knock the topic out of the way and to prevent the conversation from continuing into something deeper—and more uncomfortable.

Casuistry and platitudes are helpful for some people. For some who are struggling, it is beneficial to dismiss their thoughts with pleasant words that will help them make it through, day-by-day. For others, however, this phrase (and similar ones) can feel dismissive and avoidant of the issue. Telling someone that they *can't* kill themselves doesn't change the fact that someone *wants* to kill themselves. Even if the thoughts go away for the moment, the core issue remains unresolved, and the suicidal feelings are bound to resurface. In order to have more effective conversations and help more people, we have to create an environment tailored to the specific needs of SWIS. For many, that may include moving past this phrase. Not everyone can find comfort in such statements, and that's okay. It's important that we recognize that the things we may have learned are "good" to say might be causing more harm than good. This is why it is so important to initiate individual conversations with people who are suicidal and learn what works best for them.

We need to start talking about how we can encourage people to live by helping them find reasons to *want* to, as opposed to trying to convince them that they *have* to. It's important that we acknowledge that suicide is a very real option, whether we like it or not. If it weren't, we wouldn't have lost so many people to this tragedy. In ignoring this fact, we are more likely to ignore important signs that SWIS needs support.

Asking "Why?"

Over the decade that I've been battling suicidal thoughts and teaching myself not to be ashamed of them, I've progressively opened up to more people about my struggles. A lot of the time, the first response I get is to ask "why?" It's a question that often leaves me stumped. I don't often think about why I'm suicidal. I don't have time to worry about that "why" when I'm busy constantly fighting either for my life or to end it. All I know is that there's a feeling in me that tells me that fighting is not worth it.

There are a number of reasons that can contribute to someone feeling suicidal: a chemical imbalance, financial/environmental/situational struggles, lacking basic necessities, daily physical and emotional struggles, chronic illness or pain, expensive medical needs and no healthcare, abuse, neglect, lacking access to therapy or medicine, therapy or medicine that isn't working, racial tension/racism, sexism, homophobia/transphobia, feeling trapped into parenthood/adulthood, etc. The list of reasons can go on for a long time, but the "why" is not what really matters. What matters is the experience of SWIS.

Professionals are best equipped to take the answers SWIS gives to "why?" and turn them into tools that help that person to get better. Even if you aren't a professional, you can still learn how to navigate the conversation. Asking someone "why" they're suicidal is almost always a precursor to trying to remedy the situation, and it is a trap. Some people get caught up in wanting to fix the things in the world that make people suicidal, as opposed to encouraging individuals to live. Instead of trying to help the person in front of them, they seek a mass reparation of the never-ending societal battle with suicide. Beyond the fact that magically fixing all of the bad things in the world is unrealistic, even if you could rid the world of all the painful, negative, and unhappy things, there would still be people who are suicidal. Some people just really want to die and will never be able to put the "why" into words.

As much as this is sad to think about, it's important that we recognize it. We need to be there for loved ones who need our support on their journey to healing, and we need to facilitate spaces in which SWIS feels comfortable asking for the help they need. We also need to keep a dialogue going about what conversations are helpful to have and which conversations aren't. It's important that the people who are struggling with suicidal thoughts are always at the center of the conversation— not old research, not what the pastor teaches, not even the information given in this book. The best way to learn how to help someone is to ask.

PART TWO

NAVIGATING CONVERSATIONS ABOUT SUICIDE

Starting the Conversation with Care

I've talked a lot about people having these conversations the wrong way, and you may be thinking, "what is the right way?" Over the years, I've had many harmful conversations with people who claim that they were trying to help me. I recently realized that as a society, we don't have any resources that talk about suicidal thoughts in a way that is helpful—how could I expect people to know any better?

In this chapter, I've compiled a list of my least favorite tactics that people use when talking about suicide and why they are harmful. This isn't by any means an exhaustive list, but it'll get the conversation going.

General Tips

In order to get a better idea of how to properly navigate these conversations, let's first go over some general guidance.

- **Handle Discussions with Care:** Don't handle these conversations with kid gloves. Many suicidal people don't like being coddled like wounded animals. It is important to remember that someone telling you that they are suicidal doesn't fundamentally change who they are as a person, and it can make them feel isolated to be treated differently after sharing their struggles with you. These conversations don't need to be navigated by walking on eggshells. It's equally important that you don't handle the discussion with reckless abandon. Show sensitivity during these conversations, but keep in mind that it's just like any other important conversation you've had with that person. Let them lead and offer your support wherever you can.

- **Regulate Yourself First:** Trying to have a conversation with someone who is dysregulated (in this case someone who is struggling with suicidal thoughts) is impossible if you are also dysregulated. Calming someone else down while you are freaking out is an impossible task. I can guarantee that you aren't going to make any progress. It's important that you always take time to focus on how you are feeling before and during the conversation, and that you maintain active communication throughout. If you feel overwhelmed, let the other person know that you need to take some time before having this conversation. If you feel better later, you can go back to conversation then. If not, then you can let the person know that you can only help them from a distance because you are also struggling with something and/or don't feel equipped to help them. Most importantly, make sure to take the steps necessary to take care of your own mental health. *Your* health always comes first. Don't prioritize their struggles over your own, as it is only going to lead to resentment and dysfunction in your relationship with them. Deciding to be a support system for someone who is experiencing suicidal thoughts is a very kind thing to do. However, it can quickly become harmful to SWIS if you don't remember to check in with yourself.

• **Prepare to Listen to the Problem, Not Try to Solve it Right Away:** Never go into these conversations expecting to "talk someone out of" suicide. That is an enormous amount of pressure, and it makes it a lot harder to regulate yourself. If you go in with the idea that this person is going to kill themselves if you don't come up with the perfect thing to say in this moment, it's impossible to have a meaningful dialogue. Also, if you begin with a motivation (i.e. trying to "solve" the problem that this person is suicidal) as opposed to going in with open ears and open arms, it can be harmful. Oftentimes, SWIS really just needs someone to encourage them and support them in their journey to getting the help they need. They need to know that their well-being is valuable to someone, that they will not be shamed for seeking help, and that someone is rooting for their recovery. Having someone to validate their feelings can help them feel comfortable enough to then reach out to a professional or start taking other steps toward recovery. As the person that they've reached out to for support, it is not your responsibility to solve their issues for them. Your goal should always be to make the other person feel safe to start moving toward happiness in a way that makes them feel comfortable.

- **Each Conversation is Unique:** The most important thing to remember in all of this is that everyone is an individual. So often people are seeking a be-all-end-all, step-by-step solution to suicide and to how to prevent suicidal people from dying. The search of a one-size-fits-all solution to suicide ignores the plethora of reasons that individuals begin to experience suicidal thoughts. While the knowledge that I can offer based on my personal experience might be a great place to start, these conversations need to be tailored to the individuals that are struggling. Only the individual experiencing suicidal thoughts can tell you what would make them the most comfortable and help them the most. Start by asking them what they need. Why did they decide to reach out? Do they need advice, comfort, an ear, or direction? Do they want you to help them come up with a solution? Do they want you to just give them kind words? Do they just need someone to sit and listen so they can organize their thoughts out loud, or do they need someone to sit down with them and help them decide on which therapist to try first? In every instance of somcone struggling with suicidal thoughts, the next step depends on the individual.

What NOT to Say

The following hypothetical situations and instructions are based on the real life experiences of myself and others who have confided in me about their challenges with people navigating these conversations poorly. This is not a step-by-step guide to these conversations, but it is information that can help you find better ways to communicate and advise what to keep in mind. It might take some practice and adjustment, but it will be worth it to know that you have done your best to support SWIS that you care about.

This section isn't meant to be read like an algebra textbook, where you accept everything you read as universal fact. It is meant to make you think deeper about the ways that you would currently navigate these hypothetical situations, and then to tell you why they may or may not be harmful—all while giving you the tools to handle these conversations in real life. Ideally, it will give you a better understanding of what someone who is suicidal is actually looking for in a conversation about their struggles. Remember not to become robotic with your dialogue or present this knowledge to SWIS as if you know better than they do. Implement the tips that I give in your own way, so that you don't sound like you've memorized flashcards or come across as disconnected from the conversation.

| 1 |

"It gets better."

Navigation with Delusion or (Internet) Clichés

Don't tell SWIS "It gets better", "But think of the beaches you'll never get to see", or "If you die now, you'll miss out on all of the good things in store for you." While some might find these phrases give them hope and a reason to keep going, many people with persistent thoughts of suicide (like myself), have heard these very general, false promises many times before. And they aren't ever helpful.

Not too long ago, I saw an Instagram post that was being shared around titled "100 Reasons Not to Kill Yourself." It was the perfect example of this flawed method of navigation. Some of the reasons listed included "It's possible to turn frowns upside down", "Being alive is just really good", "What about food? You'll miss chocolate and all the other nom things!", and some items as simple as "Stargazing", "Trampolines", and "Starbucks"... as standalone reasons not to die. Listing off human behaviors and physical items that might help someone to experience joy is not a remedy for someone's suicidal thoughts. Many people who are suicidal lead fairly normal lives and are able to partake in exciting activities. They experience moments of joy and happiness, look at the stars, eat chocolate, and "smile every day", but those distractions don't address the bigger issue. Those brief moments of pleasure don't negate the lack of a desire to keep living. It's like putting a Band-Aid on a broken bone: completely irrelevant and unhelpful.

SWIS and has been struggling with suicidal thoughts for an extended period of time is likely long past the time when these cliche ideas could have helped them in any way, shape, or form. We know that things don't just get better for no reason. We might feel that life is inherently purposeless and lack the desire to create purpose for ourselves. And as much as Starbucks is delicious, we know that frozen caramel drinks aren't going to hold us over for another forty years. This method of navigation hinges on the idea that suicidal people have nothing to be happy about, as opposed to the idea that suicidal people feel that the things they are struggling with outweigh any happiness they currently feel or have the potential to feel.

Let's put this into an example so that we can get a better idea of how it comes across to people who are suicidal when you use this method of navigation:

Matthew and Todd are best friends. Recently, Matthew has been struggling with thoughts of suicide and doesn't know who else to turn to. Matthew opens up to Todd about his struggles, telling him that he has been experiencing suicidal thoughts since several things in his life have not been going well. He lost his job, he is at risk of eviction, and he just got a notice saying that he might lose his car soon. After listening to his best friend bare his struggles in search of some support, Todd tells Matthew that "things always get better" and suggests that Matthew should "try harder to focus on the bright side of things." Matthew is left feeling like his struggles have been disregarded, because Todd didn't actually address a single thing that came out of Matthew's mouth. Matthew knows that there is no bright side to not knowing where his next meal will come from, where he will sleep if he gets evicted, or where he'll keep his things if his car is taken. Todd not only diminished the feelings and fears of his best friend when he said that Matthew should simply try harder to see the good, but he also completely shut down the conversation with this statement. "Look at the bright side" does not allow for any further conversation without it seeming like Matthew is trying to argue with Todd's point of view.

A much more effective approach Todd could have taken would have been to address each point that Matthew shared (his job, his risk of eviction, and his risk of losing his car) to ensure he felt heard and supported.

Todd should have given individual weight to each thing that Matthew said. For example, saying "I'm really sorry that you lost your job, and I hope that it doesn't come to eviction." When the struggles are addressed individually, as opposed to in a big lump, it can help SWIS to feel that you were actually listening. In my experience, people tend to summarize when I start sharing my struggles. I will say something along the lines of "I've recently been struggling with my self-worth, and I'm experiencing a lot of hopelessness. I can't really find motivation to do much anymore, because I feel like nothing I do is important." When someone responds with something like, "Just hang in there. It'll get better," it seems that all the other person hears is "I'm sad." In reality, I communicated three distinct struggles that I was having, all that have a separate effect on me, and will send me down separate paths as I begin to heal from them. "Just think of how pretty the beach is!" can feel incredibly dismissive of the conversation that SWIS is trying to have with you. If SWIS was looking for understanding from this conversation, it can be hard for them to feel that they have a supportive audience or that they've adequately gotten their point across when they are given a phrase that is so general and conditional that it has largely lost its meaning.

Offering assistance can be really helpful both in giving the listener a way to respond and also helping SWIS to know that they've been heard. When faced with a situation such as "I might be evicted" or "I might lose my car", it's not realistic for the listener to say, "I will help you pay your bills." But assistance doesn't always equate to solving the issue. Even something as simple as "I'll be on the lookout for job interviews for you," or "I'll be sure to ask my boss if they have connections at a different location," or "If I see any ads for a cheaper apartment I'll let you know," could be very helpful. It lets the person know that someone has got their back and wants to help them, and it can help them feel less hopeless in the moment.

When faced with a struggle that you don't know how to offer assistance for, it's still important to address it. Saying something as simple as "I hear you. I can't imagine what you must be going through," can be helpful. (Make sure your tone does not come across as disingenuous.) It lets them know that you were listening and that you're coming from a place of kindness and honesty. Someone saying that to me makes me feel understood and supported enough to take the next step toward healing.

It's important to recognize that SWIS is being extremely emotionally vulnerable with you, and it has probably taken a lot of courage for them to open up to you. Not only have they been struggling with these thoughts and feelings long enough and seriously enough to reach out for help, but it can be really hard to put what they're struggling with into words. If they can take the time, effort, and emotional energy to ask you for help, the least you can do is offer them an honest, thought-out response. Tell them how you feel, even if you aren't sure of the most helpful response. Something along the lines of, "That was hard to hear. I have no clue what to say," or "Hearing that you feel that way really hurts. Let me know if there's anything I can do," can help them to feel like you're engaging in the conversation. I've had people tell me that they cling to delusion and internet clichés not only because they're easy, but because they feel like a "safe" response. Some people fear messing up during these conversations, but trying to walk on eggshells is worse. Allow yourself the space to mess up and allow SWIS the space to redirect you if you've caused them harm. Fear shouldn't be the thing that drives these conversations. We should be seeking connection and understanding.

Many people have told me that I'm being stubborn for not allowing any mentions of "it gets better" in my space. My breakdown of why that's not helpful has offended some people, and they've insisted that I don't want to get better. That kind of ignorance is really harmful to me. I want nothing more than to get better. Healing is my top priority at all times, but it's equally important to me that I don't compromise on who I am or what I believe for the sake of getting better. I've tried that before, and it's structurally weak. Every attempt at wellness built on the underpinning of trying to be someone that I am not has crumbled within a month. No one should have to fundamentally change who they are in order to feel good about life. It's harmful to insist that because you don't have the tools to help someone, or because someone doesn't like the tools that you're offering as help, that they are choosing to remain suicidal.

| 2 |

"Don't be selfish."

Navigation with Guilt

I recently received a DM from a good friend of mine recommending a TV show that he really enjoyed. He asked me to watch it and get back to him about whether or not I liked it. I told him that I would. The next couple of weeks were especially tough in terms of struggling with my suicidal thoughts, and in the constant battle of attacking and defending myself, the TV show completely slipped my mind. About three weeks later, he messaged me again, asking for my thoughts. I can't say that I was doing *well* at that point, but I was on my way to feeling a little better. I apologized for not watching the show yet and, to avoid him thinking that I simply didn't want to watch, I briefly mentioned the fact that I struggle with suicidal thoughts and that the past couple weeks had especially sucked. I assured him that I'd still love to watch the show when I was feeling better. He asked me to delve deeper into what I said about being suicidal and insisted that he wanted to be an ear for me and what I was going through. Per his request, I gave some more details but insisted that I was going to be fine, and that the conversation did not need to continue. I assume he, like most people that rope me into these discussions, felt an obligation to talk about it. Some people think they should be "doing something" when it comes to mentions of suicide, or think that suicidal people need a "talking to." Ironically, these thoughts often lead to navigating conversations poorly.

Despite my earlier insistence that I was going to be okay and didn't need to talk about it more, he still offered me a few clichés. When I explained to him why those were not helpful, I seemed to set something off. He immediately started belittling me and my struggles, calling me things like "shortsighted" and "pretentious." Then he pulled out the classic "you're selfish." The last thing I read before I put the conversation on mute was him saying that I "know better" than to feel the feelings I feel, and to have the experiences that I have. Needless to say, the conversation didn't end very well. I had tried to get in and out of the conversation with brevity and honesty because I wasn't feeling well, but I felt like he had tricked me into experiencing something that made me feel a thousand times worse.

This is the perfect example of navigation with guilt, which most commonly sounds like "How selfish of you," or "How could you do that to your parents/friends/coworkers/dog/plants?" or "So you're telling me that I don't matter enough for you not to kill yourself?" Let's look at an example:

Sam and Jaden are siblings. Sam opens up to Jaden for the first time about how they've been struggling with suicidal thoughts. Sam says that the pain they've been dealing with has become too much to bear, and now they feel like dying is the way that they'd like to solve their problems. Jaden hears this and starts listing off the names of all the people Sam knows. "Mom, Dad, Granny, Papa, Steven, Latrice, and Josh...do those people just mean nothing to you? What are we supposed to do without you?" he asks.

In Sam's time of need, Jaden wants Sam to know just how much harm they will cause if they die by suicide. This leaves Sam feeling guilty for experiencing their suicidal thoughts, but it does not make the thoughts go away. Over time, Sam's suicidal thoughts only worsen, and every time they start to struggle, the pain is compounded by remembering how awful everyone thinks they are for struggling.

A much more effective approach Jaden could have taken would be to first validate Sam's feelings, instead of immediately getting defensive and making them feel guilty.

People get so combative during conversations about suicide because they think that comforting someone and offering them a safe space to talk equates to encouraging them to kill themselves. This is not the case. If SWIS tells you that they need an ear, then it's safe to assume that all they need from you is an ear. You don't need to assume that you are the deciding factor in whether they live or not. Sometimes people just need someone to tell them that they care while they sort their thoughts out loud. If SWIS expresses that they disagree with something you've said, it doesn't mean that they're trying to get you to agree with them. They're trying to communicate the disconnect between the two of you and explain why the things you're saying are simply not helpful (or even blatantly harmful) for them to hear. You needn't prepare a court case for why they shouldn't kill themselves. You can validate their feelings by recognizing the pain they are in, and not making them feel bad for being in pain. Tell them that you can see how deeply it's affecting them, and that it's understandable to not want to be in pain.

It is invalidating, for example, to tell someone that they shouldn't be feeling the way that they feel. Validating the feelings of SWIS can set the stage for a smooth, meaningful dialogue that will be infinitely more helpful than making them feel guilty and burdensome for reaching out for help.

I've heard SLN argue that when they use this guilt method of navigation, their true intent is to make sure that SWIS knows that they are loved. If that is your true intent, a more effective way of getting that point across is by telling someone that they and their feelings are valid and important to you. In the above example, Sam glossed over the idea of feeling a lot of pain and not knowing what to do with that pain. If Jaden had created a safe space for Sam, Sam might have felt comfortable enough to dive deeper into the specifics of what they're struggling with. This specificity would be beneficial to both SLN and SWIS, as it can help them come up with the next step to take, be that therapy, a doctor's appointment, or even a change in workload.

There have been so many times that people, after learning that I struggle with suicidal thoughts, share with me an intimate story about someone who died by suicide at some point in their life. I usually appreciate that people feel comfortable enough to share those things with me—unless their goal is not mutual support, but making me feel guilty. I can tell the difference: some people share because they have a deep personal connection and want me to know that they care about me, and some people bring up a story in order to instill shame or guilt. When SLN does the latter, they seem to be of the belief that I am suicidal because I think that nobody cares about me, so they tell me a vague story of someone who died and is deeply missed. I know (and have been told countless times) that so many people would miss me if I ever died by suicide. I know that I've affected people's lives in ways that I will never fully understand, and all of the other kindly clichés that people toss around. But it doesn't change the fact that I'm suicidal. Hounding SWIS about how they'd be destroying other people's lives if they died by suicide will not help them. They'll just feel even worse.

Kindness, compassion, and honesty are the best route to take with these conversations. Remember, your goal as SLN is always to help SWIS feel supported enough to get themselves help.

| 3 |

"You just want attention."

Navigation by Centering Yourself, Rather Than SWIS

As SLN, navigating a conversation about suicide by putting yourself at the center of it is never going to be effective. SLN will use this method of navigation most often when talking to a third party about SWIS. It can sound like "she just wants attention," or "misery loves company." One evening, I was on FaceTime with my younger sister and a friend of hers. This friend begins lamenting to us about his ex and how awful it was to date her. A generally funny conversation about avoiding an obsessive and manipulative ex became confusing when he said, "I would never date a suicidal girl again."

I asked him where that came from, and he said, "That girl, my ex that I was just telling you about, she was suicidal."

"I mean, I got that, but what does her being suicidal have to do with her being a bad person?" I asked.

"You know how misery loves company. She was so suicidal that when she saw that I cared about her, she latched onto that and since she knew I was happy, she had to do anything she could to ruin it. That misery really rubs off on you."

As the conversation continued, it became clear that his issue didn't lie so much in the way that she was dealing with her suicidal thoughts, but in the fact that she was suicidal to begin with. He—like many others—had preconceived notions about people who struggle with suicidal thoughts, including the idea that SWIS and confides in others has some ulterior motive. It was clear that every theory he had about his ex's actions was rooted in this idea that suicidal people behave with an intention to take direct action against others. This is the main thing that causes people to use this method of navigation.

Let's take a look at this hypothetical situation:

Essence has a history of suicidal thoughts. Her friend, Laureen, told Essence that it was okay to confide in her, in the case that she needed someone to talk to. After a few conversations about Essence's state and her struggles with suicide, Laureen became overwhelmed with the things Essence was telling her. The next time Essence tried to confide in Laureen, Laureen said, "I get that you're suicidal, but you don't have to suck the life out of everything around you. Just because you're sad doesn't mean the rest of us have to be."

Essence was left broken, confused, and feeling burdensome. From then on, Essence had trouble trusting other people enough to disclose her troubles, even when she was a danger to herself. She also began to doubt herself and her feelings. She worried that expressing her struggles would only cause harm to others, and she knew that other people would believe she was only reaching out for attention.

A much more effective approach Laureen could have taken would have been to explain that she was overwhelmed without placing the blame for her own feelings on Essence.

After agreeing to be an ear for SWIS, it is so important that you constantly check in with yourself about your own well-being, so as not to blindside yourself or the other person with your anxieties. Providing such a service can be draining, and it is perfectly understandable and okay to take a break. Your own mental health should always be your top priority. The problem begins when SLN starts to place blame onto SWIS for the fact that they are becoming overwhelmed.

When Laureen said, "I get that you're suicidal, but you don't have to suck the life out of everything around you," she implied that Essence has control over the way sharing her struggles affect the people around her. Was there anything that Essence could have done to not "suck the life out of" Laureen, or was Laureen feeling understandably upset and drained after hearing intimate details of her friend's battle with suicide? When Laureen agreed to be an ear for Essence, she may not have known just how emotionally taxing it would be to do so. But Essence wasn't in the wrong for being honest about how deeply she was struggling. Essence committed no fault or wrongdoing to warrant blame in the way that Laureen is assigning it. Laureen gave Essence permission to confide in her. While no one is "at fault" in this situation, Laureen's failure to communicate the fact that she needed a break from supporting is her responsibility and hers alone. It is not fair of her to put the onus on Essence. Furthermore, Laureen's statement that "just because you're sad doesn't mean the rest of us have to be," implies that she believes Essence intends to make other people sad when she confides in them.

Suicidal people don't feed off the sadness and fear of their loved ones like some demon in a horror movie. Sometimes, SWIS just needs to share their feelings with someone else so they don't feel trapped inside their own head. If you offer to be an ear for SWIS, it is not their responsibility to monitor your well-being and your ability to handle those conversations. As SLN, you would be doing yourself a disservice to not be honest about how these conversations are negatively affecting your mental health. If you become overwhelmed, or if you enter a place in your life where you no longer have the capacity to listen, it is your duty to yourself to communicate that—and their duty to you to respect it.

In this situation, Laureen centering her own experience in this conversation about suicide caused her to navigate the situation in a way that was harmful to Essence. If you remember that suicidal people should always be the center of conversations about suicide, it will automatically pave the way for more effective methods of navigation.

Instead of saying, "You're sucking the life out of me," Laureen could have said, "This is taking a lot out of me, emotionally." Instead of "Just because you're sad doesn't mean everyone else has to be," she could have tried, "It really hurts to see you struggle so much." The difference may seem miniscule, but the intent, the angle of approach, and the connotation of the words used all simultaneously play a role in the impact your words have on SWIS.

As SWIS, this method of navigation makes me feel like I don't have any real safe spaces. There have been so many instances in which someone has insisted that it was okay for me to confide in them, only to go behind my back and roll their eyes with someone else, talking about how annoying I am. Sometimes people learning to navigate insist that SWIS has a friend in them, a support system, or an ear because they feel obligated to do so. But remember, you never have to let SWIS confide in you, no matter how distraught they seem to be, and no matter how much it's been ingrained in you that reluctantly agreeing to listen will save them. That is not your responsibility. That is not fair to you, nor SWIS, as you are bound to snap at some point—and that is infinitely more harmful than helpful. It might be a little bit disappointing for SWIS to learn that they've overwhelmed you, but it will encourage them to find someone who is better equipped to support them on their journey to professional help and eventually healing.

In not being completely in touch and honest with themselves about their feelings, SLN may try to rationalize where those feelings stem from by blaming SWIS. When they go on to navigate a conversation about suicide by centering themselves, SLN begins to see SWIS as the villain. This can sound like, "You want to hang out all of the time! I guess misery really does love company," and "Nothing is wrong with you! This is just a desperate attempt to get everyone to pay attention to you!"

Misery is not a character trait, and SWIS is not the antagonist in this story. Checking in with yourself before accepting someone else's troubles into your life will help to eliminate this pattern of pain during conversations about suicide.

| 4 |

"Just kill yourself, then. You won't."

Navigation with Dismissal and Misunderstanding

Navigations with dismissal and misunderstanding are two distinct methods, but they have very similar suggestions for better approaches, so I've combined them in this section. Let's start by exploring navigation with dismissal first.

Navigation with Dismissal

This method of navigation involves trying to shut down a conversation about suicide, especially due to a belief that someone reaching out for help means that they aren't going to harm themselves. If they really wanted to harm themselves, they would have done it already. This goes back to the misconception that suicidal people "don't actually want to kill themselves." Those using this method were likely told that most people who die by suicide don't ever reach out for help. It is also commonly believed that if you reach out for help, that is proof that you "don't actually want to die." This can be better explained through an example:

Raegan and Cletus are having an uncomfortable conversation about Cletus' suicidal thoughts. Raegan gave Cletus permission to confide in her about some suicidal feelings he's been struggling with for a while. Cletus says he feels like his life is purposeless and that he can't seem to find a reason to want to go on. He tells her that he knows that people would miss him if he died, but he also feels that his pain is too much to handle, and he can't just wait until he finds some purpose.

Raegan, frustrated by what she sees as Cletus "being negative", says, "If you were really going to kill yourself, you wouldn't have come to me to stop you, right? You know that what you're saying isn't true, so why are we talking about this right now? Stop being dramatic." Cletus is left feeling like his struggles aren't important or worth reaching out to someone about. Not only did Raegan's response exacerbate his feelings of purposelessness, but her dismissal of the issue can be dangerous if Cletus ever becomes an imminent danger to himself and no longer tries to reach out for help. Cletus feels defeated.

A much more effective approach Raegan could have taken would have been to take Cletus' concerns seriously and realize that his reaching out for help does not indicate that he isn't (or won't become) a danger to himself.

When SLN implies that SWIS reaching out for help eliminates the possibility of them dying by suicide, it diminishes the struggles and pain that they are experiencing. As much as reaching out for help might be a step in fighting to survive, it doesn't mean that SWIS will no longer attempt suicide just because they've tried one of many approaches that can help. This is especially true when reaching out for help is ineffective, much like Reagan and Cletus' conversation was. Whether she dismissed his concerns because she felt overwhelmed, frustrated, or just genuinely believed that there was nothing to worry about, Reagan separated herself from the conversation by trying to convince Cletus that his problems weren't serious enough to talk about.

Navigation with Misunderstanding

Navigation with misunderstanding happens when SLN believes that SWIS is exacerbating their own problems by refusing to take a step SLN believes is painfully simple or obvious (e.g. going to therapy, following through with the desire to attempt suicide, or not thinking about it). This can sound like "Just kill yourself, then," or "Well, then just get help," or "You're choosing to remain suicidal by continuing to talk about it."

Here's an example:

Deon and Oscar are talking about their recent troubles in life. Deon opens up to Oscar about his suicidal thoughts. He tells Oscar that he's been struggling with suicidal thoughts for a few years, now. Deon says that at the beginning he had a lot of hope that it would get better, but now he doesn't feel that way anymore. Oscar responds by saying, "Well, you're sitting here wasting time and talking to me when you could be in therapy figuring it out. I think that you just like being sad." Deon is left feeling like his struggles are inconsequential to Oscar, and that he has been misunderstood. Oscar believes that Deon is not trying hard enough, but Deon knows that the distance he's come has required him to fight tooth and nail.

A much more effective approach Oscar could have taken would have been to not assume anything about the situation or assume that his suggestions will be automatically helpful to Deon.

Oscar insists that Deon is wasting his time by reaching out to a friend instead of a therapist. Remember that therapy is not readily accessible to everyone, especially in America. Deon may not have health insurance that covers therapy. If he does have insurance, it may have a very limited network of covered mental health-care providers and an expensive copay. For all Oscar knows, Deon could already be actively attending therapy. Oscar has this idea that therapy "fixes" suicidal thoughts, but he really has little to no grasp on what that process looks like or what that entails. This is an example of SLN misunderstanding the process that it takes to heal and assuming they have the answer.

In both examples, the conversation could have been better navigated if SLN (Oscar and Raegan) accepted the fact that SWIS (Deon and Cletus) had a different perspective. In both situations, Oscar and Raegan said very harmful things under the veil of sincerity. Both navigation by dismissal and navigation by misunderstanding hinge on SLN insisting that they have an earnest suggestion and feeling vindicated when SWIS does not have a ready response to it.

It's important to understand the difference between a genuine sentiment and a challenge. A genuine sentiment, such as "Why haven't you tried therapy?" or "What do you think your reason to keep going is?" is acceptable in these conversations, as SLN is asking for clarification, a different perspective, and further understanding. If SLN is presenting a challenge, those same questions turn into: "Why haven't you tried therapy?" and "Well, why don't you just kill yourself?" The difference lies in the intention. A genuine inquiry seeks to deepen the conversation while a challenge seeks to separate SLN from the conversation. A challenge assumes the conversation is an argument, and they can "win" with their suggestion.

If Oscar and Raegan knew the difference between these two situations and made an effort not to abuse this understanding (i.e. not gaslighting someone by insisting that they meant something genuinely when they didn't), they would have been more helpful to Cletus and Deon. Oscar challenged Deon by saying he was wasting time by talking to him, and Raegan challenged Cletus by claiming he was not going to kill himself. When you view a conversation about suicide as an argument, no one wins. You leave SWIS feeling belittled and defeated—and still suicidal.

Reagan and Oscar should have accepted that they're not going to agree with everything that Deon and Cletus are saying. Sometimes, SWIS says things that are hard to hear, or things that—to someone who doesn't struggle with suicidal thoughts—sound absolutely ridiculous. When SLN decides that they want to "win" a conversation about suicide, they assume they can convince SWIS to think differently about a feeling that they've expressed. This is never productive. This goes back to the universal desire to just "prevent suicide," instead of also remedying the reasons people die by suicide. If we learn to accept SWIS's experience for what it is and work *with* them instead of *against* them, we'll make much more progress in this battle against suicide.

It's also important to accept that SWIS is not always expecting a solution when opening up to SLN. Sometimes, SWIS is sharing because bottling their feelings up makes their situation worse.

There is a misconception that SWIS conveying the fact that they experience suicidal thoughts is an invitation for SLN to try and fix it, as opposed to SWIS simply expressing their pain. This can lead to SLN getting frustrated with their inability to solve or "win" the conversation, and saying things like, "Well, if you want to die so badly, why are you still alive? Why isn't every waking moment a suicide attempt for you?"

We need to start asking SWIS what is helpful to them, what their goal in healing is, and getting them into therapy as soon as possible. That is the only way that we are going to successfully encourage our loved ones and help them want to live.

A lot of people believe that because there are gaps in between my suicide attempts, that means that I don't really want to kill myself that badly or that, when I'm not actively attempting suicide, I'm not suicidal at those times. This brings up a few concepts that I'd like to talk about.

Most of the time that I open up about my decade-long struggle with suicidal thoughts, I am offering a fair forewarning before I loop someone into a friendship they're not equipped to handle. I'm telling someone a piece of information about me that is very necessary for them to know. The fact that I am suicidal has affected every walk of my life. It affects the way I plan for things, it affects my eating habits, it affects the people that I am able to keep around me, so to me, after a certain point in my relationships with people, it is very important that they know that I am suicidal. This way, it doesn't come as a surprise when I actually am reaching out for help. That being said, in these situations, I never said once that I was *going* to kill myself. I did not threaten my own life, nor was I reaching out for help. Therefore, the answer would be, "Why would you expect me to kill myself? Do you not have faith in my ability to win my battle against suicide?" I describe my relationship with suicide as a *struggle* and a *battle* because I'm constantly doing just that in trying to survive. To suggest otherwise is insensitive.

In general people lack an understanding of just how much thought goes into a suicide attempt. I often respond to "Why are you still alive then," by telling people that "suicide is impossible". Obviously, this is not true, but I do wholeheartedly believe that in order to successfully die by suicide, you have to be the perfect combination of methodical and impulsive. There are so many factors that are necessary to consider: How am I going to? Where am I going to? How much time do I have? How long until someone finds me? What if someone finds me too early and they take me to the hospital? *What would the repercussions of surviving be?*

Every time I've attempted suicide, these are just a few of the logistical questions that run through my mind, and I won't even get into the emotional questions that come with it. The repercussions of surviving are what steer me away from suicide attempts more often than not. If someone finds me mid-attempt of a "bathtub suicide", I might lose the ability to control my nondominant arm and my family won't let me use the bathroom with the door closed anymore. If I survive a "roof suicide", every bone in my body will be broken and I'll be in indescribable pain for months. If someone finds me after I've attempted a "closet suicide", then I'll have brain damage because I've lacked oxygen for too long or I'll have snapped my neck. Either way, I won't have the motor function to try again.

So, no. The driving factor in my refusal to attempt any and every way to die at all times is not rooted in some deeper, subconscious desire to stay alive. It's rooted in my knowledge that my attempt could (and based on my track record, probably will) fail and then I'd really be stuck being alive until my body gives out. People may see this as a "choice" to live. Again, we can argue semantics, but

I'd rather talk about something productive: I think a lot of the rage that is directed towards SWIS in situations similar to the afore-mentioned, stems from the very common opinion that life is some-thing that you should be eternally grateful for and try to preserve at all costs.

I am so often met with this idea that, for no other reason than the fact that you were born, you should be so happy that you are alive. "Think of how many sperm you were racing against! You fought to win!" Without needing to explain that sperm don't experience con-sciousness, it is very important to me that people start to recognize that being born is not an indisputable reason to continue to live, and you cannot convince someone that their struggles are not real because you see death as a worse outcome. To get into this topic, it needs to be acknowledged that not a single person chose to be born. Even the people who love every second of their life, and always have, are just a product of their parents' desire for them to live, and sometimes not even that. Sadly, it is still very common that people will open up about their suicidal thoughts to someone they trust and be met with responses such as "How can you be suicidal? You have clothes, food, and water. You go to a nice school. You have the newest smartphone." I've heard this most often from parents.

With every new person that is born into this world, there is another dice rolling of whether or not that person will be mentally well. When an individual decides to have children, they should have a deep understanding that the child does not owe them gratitude for *their* decision to give birth to the child that they decided they wanted. There is always a chance that someone will become un-happy with the life they were born into, and that is a gamble that parents take with their children's lives. I bring that up to say that no one owes anyone else happiness about the things that cause them pain in life, especially in the context of wishing for a way out of a life they are unhappy with. This fight to convince SWIS that their struggles are not so bad or aren't worth remedying because there will always be someone that has it worse is counterproductive if the goal is to encourage somebody to live. The focus on convincing suicidal people that they shouldn't be suicidal (or in some cases, trying to convince them that they just aren't suicidal) instead of offering them support to help them find their own way to a corner of life that makes them happy and comfortable is why so many people see suicide as either the best or the only option.

Living is inactive. Dying requires action. Despite what Lin-Manuel said, living is easy and dying is harder. That is to say that existing in the physical state of being alive, NOT the subsequent experiences, responsibilities, and mental turmoil, is easy, and finding a way to successfully escape the physical state of living is harder. The thought and effort required to die by suicide effectively is what keeps a lot of people alive. I insist to everyone that I am always suicidal. Even on the best days of my life, the fact that I struggle with suicidal thoughts so heavily does not just float away from me for a few days at a time. However, when my suicidal thoughts are not especially hard to fight, I think of the things that are important to me. My little brother and little sister are infinitely more important to me than how badly I want to die. My best friends, my old teachers, my desire to follow my dreams, my desire to own four cats one day, my desire to eat more butter pecan ice-cream, are all infinitely more important to me than how badly I want to die, when I'm having a good day. The problem lies in the fact that, as the days become worse, as the metaphorical skies become more gray, those things that were so obviously so much more important to me than my desire to die start to float away. All of a sudden, I don't know what matters more to me. When that line starts to blur is when I am most dangerous to myself. If that violent fluctuation of my mental state goes on to be put aside indefinitely, I can never say for certain that I will still be here tomorrow. The fear that comes with that pushes people away. The less support I have, the harder it is for me to get better and the harder it becomes for people to stick around, and the cycle continues on. That is why suicidal thoughts need to be addressed. That is why it doesn't help SWIS when you tell them to think about their favorite foods and the people that they love the most when they are in the middle of a crisis. Oftentimes, as my brain exists in the turmoil and fog of a crisis, those things become meaningless to me.

| 5 |

"Oh Wise One"

Navigation by Insisting You Have the Answer

"You don't need medication! Medicine is something that was invented by the government to steal our money and control our brains!"

"You need to start meditating."

"You're only depressed because your aura is blue. You should focus on that, instead."

Thank you, oh wise soul, who insists that they know the ins and outs of my struggles with suicide so much better than I do. What I am labeling the "Oh Wise One" method happens when SLN believes that SWIS's path to healing is not good enough, and that their own beliefs, opinions, and experience are better.

I recently had a conversation with an acquaintance of mine about how my struggles with suicidal thoughts have greatly shaped my worldview. He brought up a theory of his: "I used to live in the desert," he told me. "And when I was there, I was also feeling suicidal. When I moved (to a more humid climate), I immediately felt so much better. You're probably not actually suicidal. You just think you are because your body is just trying to cope with the change in climate. Get a humidifier, and you'll feel so much better."

I tried to kindly explain to him that I've been suicidal since I was eleven years old, and I've lived in four different states since then, each with a different climate. Not once did my struggles with suicidal thoughts go away. Despite this, he was adamant that my living in a dry climate was the reason for my suicidal thoughts, and that I'm only choosing unhappiness the longer I wait to get a humidifier.

The Oh Wise One method of navigation is harmful in a similar way to navigation with misunderstanding—they both trivialize the struggles of SWIS. SLN is ignorant of the fact that SWIS will *always* be more knowledgeable than anyone else about what is helpful for them.

Here's an example:

Jade excitedly tells her best friend, Reggie, that she has finally gotten the courage to start therapy and medication to help with her suicidal thoughts. She tells him that her first session was a few months ago and she's on her way to pick up her new prescription right now. Reggie used to struggle with suicidal thoughts himself and has been Jade's biggest supporter throughout her battle. She expects him to be just as excited as she is. Instead, Reggie asks Jade why she would do something like that.

"I can't believe they got you," Reggie tells her. "They're going to tell you that something is wrong with you, and nothing is wrong with you. Everyone feels the way you do. If you start relying on someone else to solve your problems for you, can you really say that you were the one that got through it? Therapy is for the weak. Only you have the answers."

Jade is left disappointed, shut down, and feeling like there is no hope for her to ever feel better. While Reggie had no ill intent, the method of navigation that he chose was still harmful to his best friend.

A much more effective approach Reggie could have taken would have been to congratulate Jade on taking an exciting step toward healing. Even if he doesn't agree with her choice to attend therapy and take medication, he can still be supportive by focusing on Jade's feelings and experience rather than his own.

In most cases of SLN using the Oh Wise One method of navigation, the intent is to help SWIS by sharing their beliefs regarding what is and is not effective. However, this most often harms SWIS, no matter what SLN was *trying* to do. In Jade and Reggie's case, Reggie completely shattered Jade's pride in the step she'd taken and insisted that what Jade was doing was unrealistic and ineffective. Not only did this instill seeds of self-doubt in Jade about her ability to decide for herself what steps to take toward healing, but it also caused her to second guess a significant decision she'd already made.

When SWIS decides that therapy is something they're interested in, the process of collecting the necessary funds, finding the right therapist, and even physically typing the email when reaching out to the therapist can all be huge hurdles. Completing each is a significant accomplishment, and it's really harmful to diminish SWIS's pride in the achievement because of your own beliefs. No matter your personal feelings on the step that SWIS has taken toward healing, it is really important that you make sure that they know that no matter how it happens, their healing is your main concern. This is not to be confused with encouraging *every* coping mechanism that

SWIS uses. Coping mechanisms, to my understanding, can be anything that is used to help someone alleviate the pain of dealing with a problem. Many coping mechanisms are unhealthy and should not be applauded or encouraged. Steps toward healing are actions taken to remedy the problem at the root, which is healthier for SWIS.

If Reggie decided that he wasn't okay with the fact that Jade was going to therapy and starting medication—even if it meant that she would be on her way to getting better—he should have reevaluated his motives in his conversation with Jade. If Reggie's goal is to successfully "sell" a way of life to Jade, then he needs to recognize that and take a step back from the conversation. Jabbing at Jade's choices and trying to convince her that they aren't good enough (in hopes that she will choose his way instead) is rooted in self-interest. Self-promotional speeches have no place in conversations about suicide. Beyond being generally unhelpful, they turn the conversation into something about you and not SWIS, making you more likely to navigate the conversation with yourself at the center.

To ensure that he didn't slip into a bad habit of talking about his personal beliefs, Reggie could have continued the conversation by asking Jade how she felt about the step she's taking. If it truly pains Reggie too much to say, "I'm happy for you," then asking her how she feels about therapy (is she is nervous about medication?), and letting her know that he wishes her the best is a wonderful way to get around it without insinuating that he agrees with her choice. When SLN immediately starts a spiel about all the reasons they disagree with SWIS's choice, it can feel like the person learning to navigate is hoping that SWIS will not have luck in their journey to healing, just so they can be proven "right." As SLN, and especially as SLN who has never struggled with suicidal thoughts before, it's very important to remember that this conversation is not about you. What you want and what you think is best does not matter more than what SWIS is comfortable with and desires. Conversations about suicide should always be had with SWIS at the center.

For SWIS, this method of navigation might be the most frustrating of them all. It seems that no matter the situation, SLN always has something to say. It's true that therapy and medication don't work for everyone, and both are not always realistic options. I would never shame someone for saying that therapy or medicine didn't work for them, so it's especially frustrating when someone tries to tell me that my experience is invalid when I explain why a new diet or an expensive crystal doesn't get me any closer to healing.

I know all too well what it feels like to be crushed when someone belittles an attempt to get better, and I never want to make anyone else feel like that. The things that help people take steps toward healing are important, whether I agree with them or not. If you insist that cutting sugar out of your diet is helping you to remedy your suicidal thoughts at the source, I don't have the qualifications to say whether or not that's true. I would never go on a spiel about how medication is the answer you're looking for. As much as I may or may not agree, the only helpful thing I can do in that situation is nod and offer my congratulations. It's important to me that I put my skepticism aside in favor of encouraging someone to keep trying. It's the only way that we can ensure that our passionate spiels about helping someone don't do more harm than good.

PART THREE

CONVERSATION TIPS FOR THOSE EXPERIENCING SUICIDAL THOUGHTS AND SEEKING SUPPORT

Making Conversations Possible to Navigate Successfully

Suicide is an incredibly complex issue. Each case of suicidal thoughts has so much to do with the individual experiencing them and their unique stories and past. There is no universal solution to suicide, and because of that, what works for one person might not work for anyone else. This makes for a longer, more frustrating process to work through, but the more that SWIS is kept at the center of these conversations and SLN's ultimate goal is to get them professional help, the less painful these conversations will be.

General Tips for SWIS

While it is always important that SLN considers the ways that their methods of navigation might be more harmful than helpful, the onus is also on people who are suicidal to make these conversations possible to navigate successfully. As SWIS, practice habits that ensure you're not causing preventable harm to someone trying their best to help you.

Ask for Permission to Address the Topic

Before even getting into a conversation with SLN about your suicidal thoughts, it's important that you ask for their consent. No matter how bad you are feeling, your suicidal thoughts are your own responsibility. That does not mean that you need to go about the journey alone, nor does it mean that you should keep quiet about them, but it's important that you don't shame SLN for making an effort or for trying to steer you to a friend or situation that will be most beneficial for the both of you.

When SWIS is struggling most heavily, it can feel like a lot to carry. I have been guilty of subconsciously seeing conversation as an outlet for my pain and wanting to unload it onto someone else. Be mindful of when your struggles are most difficult to avoid accidentally causing someone else pain while trying to lighten your own burden. Whether SLN struggles with suicidal thoughts themselves or not, everyone has their own struggles to deal with. It's unfair to expect SLN to take on your issues on top of theirs, unless they specifically say that it is okay. It's good to want someone else to understand what you're going through, especially if you feel that that is a step needed for you to start healing. It's also imperative to keep in mind that what you're going through is the most inconceivable pain for many, and no matter your intention, you have the potential to cause great harm to others if you are careless.

Remember, just because you ask politely doesn't mean that someone has to agree to listen to your struggles. SLN may decline to have the conversation with you. No matter what their reasoning is for not wanting to listen, it is your responsibility to respect it. SWIS should not demand an explanation from SLN after they deny their request to vent. The healthiest thing to do at that point is say "okay" and move on. If you take every "no" you hear personally, you may spiral and breed resentment, later taking it out on the people who truly care about you and want you to heal. "No" is a full sentence, and it works when coming from SWIS to SLN and vice versa. Accepting rejection with grace is infinitely easier said than done, but it's important that you start practicing immediately in order to advance progress in conversations about suicide. In an ideal situation, SWIS is surrounded by people who love them and want them to get better. It is important that you don't take advantage of or abuse that love.

Use Caution on Social Media

It's important that you exercise caution when posting publicly on social media about your struggles with suicidal thoughts, so as not to overwhelm the people who care about you most. I personally understand the benefit of posting about it when you're struggling. In this day and age, social media posts are the way that we've learned to feel connected to others, and in most cases, it's very effective. However, it's important to be clear about when your posts are a means of connecting with others and when they are a cry for help when you are in crisis. The simplest way to do this is by adding a clarifying sentence at the start or end of these posts (e.g. "I really need someone right now. I'm in a crisis," or, "I'm okay. This is just how I process"). To ensure you aren't imposing your pain on people without their consent, separating these posts from the rest of your feed can be another good option. Many social media platforms offer the option to specify who sees what posts on your page or feed. Collecting a small group of friends, family, or other people close to you to receive these posts can help to minimize any panic that may ensue from a public post. You can also consider creating a page that is just for you.

I know that making Instagram posts about your suicidal thoughts is frowned upon, as most see it as a desperate attempt for attention, but when done the right way, it can have genuine benefits. Social media posts have been helpful to me by functioning as a journal of sorts, recorded on an online page that *nobody* follows. Sometimes just talking about my pain (without being able to receive responses or expect them) is all that it takes for me to survive another day. For me, even posting to the void can help me to feel like I've acknowledged the pain I'm in and begin processing further. I imagine when I start therapy, having real-time accounts of what I was going through, that I can access at any time, will be helpful in processing properly.

Posting as a means of connection can be an easy way to reach out to a selected group without feeling like you're bothering anybody.

Don't Blame Someone Learning to Navigate

You shouldn't ever blame SLN for your suicidal thoughts, your suicide attempts, and/or your suicide. In general, suicidal thoughts are never the fault of an individual, but the product of mental illness and unprocessed trauma. (Please take this with a grain of salt because I am in no place to assure that not *one* case of someone experiencing suicidal thoughts was directly perpetuated by another individual.) It is important to recognize that it is unfair to blame the people learning to navigate, especially those who are genuinely trying and/or didn't know any better for making mistakes.

We need to hold people accountable for the way that their words, actions, and sometimes lack of action hurt others. Even so, this does not mean placing blame on others for as vast and nuanced a problem as suicide. We need to afford others the same patience and forgiveness in these situations that we'd like to receive.

Please acknowledge the way that certain methods of navigation are harmful to you, and do not censor yourself in doing so, but also be careful not to weaponize the weight of your suicidal thoughts and the power you know they hold over people. There is a difference between "(SLN) is the reason I attempted suicide" and "(SLN) said something harmful by accident, and my trauma made it hard to process those words. That's what I was feeling when I attempted suicide". That difference, no matter how subtle it may seem, is instrumental in making these conversations ones that people want to get better at navigating.

Don't Weaponize Your Experience or Make Threats

Threatening people who care about you with your suicidal thoughts is never going to have a positive effect on your journey towards healing—and it makes conversations about suicide impossible to navigate. In general, most of us know not to say things like "If _____, then I'm going to kill myself," but it's important that we take even further note of the power that SWIS can have over SLN who is fearful of losing a loved one, being blamed for their death, or feeling responsible for their death. SLN never has any obligation to you. In a way, that knowledge becomes your (SWIS) responsibility to enforce. For SLN, it can be very hard to determine the gravity of a situation. I've had many people express to me that they'd like a sure way to tell when someone is just reaching out for help and when someone needs to be sent to the hospital. There is no sure way for SLN to know, but SWIS can alleviate a lot of that pressure by being direct about their intentions during a conversation.

You may never question the difference between a threat to SLN and an expression of intense emotion or a joke, but there is really no way for SLN to know for sure which is which. For example, telling your significant other something along the lines of "You're the only thing that matters to me," could be seen as romantic in a situation where neither you nor your partner are suicidal. However, if you are suicide, that simple phrase can be easily misconstrued and make your significant other feel that if they were to leave, then you would kill yourself. At that point, it is your responsibility to double down on the assurance that SLN has no obligation to you. Even if you think that they know or you're pretty sure it was clear, you can never be too careful. Something as straightforward as, "I mean that romantically, not suicidally," can make a world of difference in the wellbeing of SLN. It will reassure them of their place in your life and their (lack of) responsibility and obligation.

Navigation would be so much easier if people could read our minds, but until that technology is developed, we're stuck with having to use our words to communicate important concepts such as these. Opening up about your suicidal thoughts and sharing your struggles with others comes with a lot of responsibility. As important as it is that SLN learns to communicate with sensitivity, it's equally important that SWIS does the same.

Don't Ask Someone to "Stop You"

Asking someone to stop you from killing yourself is a losing game. It is not their responsibility or their expertise, and it irrevocably raises the stakes of the conversation you're having. It's important that you, SWIS, never put someone in a position where they feel that they don't have a choice.

I understand that suicidal crises are overwhelming, and that it can be really hard to remember events that occurred after coming down from being in the thick of one (not to mention how hard it can be to feel like you are in your body during an episode of that severity). For this reason, it is important to take preventative measures during the times that you feel in control and alert. Be mindful of the signs that indicate you are about to enter a crisis episode, start practicing self-regulation and take note of the things that help you regulate, and then share this information with the people that you care about so that everyone can have an easier time navigating the situation.

If you have decided to kill yourself, there is nothing that is going to stop you. Only a physical intervention (i.e. someone holding you down) or your own mental intervention (remedying and/or soothing your suicidal thoughts) can do that. It's important that we gather information specific to our suicidal thoughts and offer it as a tool for SLN to use in the future, instead of holding it as a hostage—whether we do this consciously or not. I know that when someone is directly asking someone else to stop them from killing themselves, their conscious intention is not to manipulate. Sometimes, SWIS doesn't intend to worry or harm SLN, and only wants the comfort of knowing that someone cares and is willing to fight for them. Still, asking someone to take on that stress is really unfair.

It's so wonderful to have someone on your side who is always willing to listen to you and calm you down when you need it, but it does take an enormous toll on that person's mental health. Try to return the care they've given to you by caring for them and making sure that you don't set them up for a lifetime of guilt if you ever were to take your own life.

We are all doing the best we can. People learning to navigate and people who are suicidal are going to make mistakes. As long as everyone has the intention of recognizing, learning from, and changing the behavior that leads to making these mistakes, then we will be alright. The most important thing for everyone in these conversations is to lead with patience and kindness.

CONCLUSION

Hopefully, by the end of this book, you feel that you have a new insight into the mind of someone who is actively suicidal. My wish is for this newfound knowledge to be applied in everyday life. Suicide is something that has the potential to affect *everyone*. For every individual learning to navigate that got something out of this book, there is another suicidal individual who has been desperately waiting for someone to understand them. Use this knowledge to start a conversation with someone you love. All too often, suicide is invisible until it's too late. It truly takes a village for SWIS to survive their battle, and hopefully we will see fewer battles being lost going forward.

These conversations are difficult to have from both sides, but nobody should be expecting perfection from the other. Self-reflection, a commitment to doing better, and a willingness to make mistakes and get back up to try again is all that SWIS needs from you. What's important is that we're taking the first step in learning how to better navigate these conversations, and we're opening doors for people (like me) to share potentially life-saving information. Too often those who are suicidal are completely dismissed and written off as unreliable or incapable of having their own valid opinions. As much as it may be an emotional journey, knowing that you're doing everything you can to support SWIS will feel so rewarding.

Suicide isn't going anywhere, and this is perpetuated by the social stigma surrounding it and by how ineffectively these conversations are currently being navigated. I hope that with the tools presented in this book, we can work to eliminate the stigma surrounding suicide, and in turn, take the step towards healing that hundreds of thousands of people lost to suicide did not have the luxury of taking. If we make the world around SWIS a safer, more understanding place, then they at least will have a fighting chance.

I hope to see some important conversations being had in the near future, and I really hope that we can collectively make a difference. We all have to do our part if we really want to put a stop to the rising suicide rates.

All of that starts with a conversation.

REFERENCES

Suicide Prevention Hotlines:

National Suicide Prevention Lifeline (U.S.)

- Phone: 1-800-273-8255 (or 988)
- Website: suicidepreventionlifeline.org
- 24/7 free and confidential support for people in distress.

Crisis Text Line (U.S. and International)

- Text: HOME to 741741
- Website: crisistextline.org
- Provides free, 24/7 crisis support via text.

Samaritans (U.K.)

- Phone: 116 123
- Website: samaritans.org
- 24/7 emotional support for people struggling to cope.

Lifeline (Australia)

- Phone: 13 11 14
- Website: lifeline.org.au
- Crisis support and suicide prevention services.

International Association for Suicide Prevention (IASP)

- Website: iasp.info
- A global directory of suicide prevention hotlines and services.

Mental Health Resources:

NAMI (National Alliance on Mental Illness)

- Website: nami.org
- Support, education, and advocacy for individuals living with mental illness.

Mental Health America (MHA)

- Website: mhanational.org
- Offers resources, screenings, and advocacy for mental health support.

Therapy Finder

- Psychology Today's Therapist Directory: psychologytoday.com
- BetterHelp: betterhelp.com
- Access to professional therapy and counseling services.

The Trevor Project (LGBTQ Youth Support)

- Phone: 1-866-488-7386
- Text: START to 678678
- Website: thetrevorproject.org
- 24/7 crisis intervention and suicide prevention for LGBTQ youth.

National Eating Disorders Association (NEDA)

- Phone: 1-800-931-2237
- Website: nationaleatingdisorders.org
- Resources and support for those affected by eating disorders.

Additional Resources:

7 Cups (Online Emotional Support)

- Website: 7cups.com
- Free, anonymous, and confidential online text chat with trained listeners.

To Write Love on Her Arms (TWLOHA)

- Website: twloha.com
- A non-profit providing hope and support for people struggling with addiction, depression, self-harm, and suicide.

The Jed Foundation (JED)

- Website: jedfoundation.org
- Promotes emotional health and prevents suicide among teens and young adults.

First-time author Brianna Valentine was born in Chicago, Illinois and raised in a nearby suburb called Homewood. She began to struggle with her mental health—and eventually suicidal thoughts—at a very early age. A combination of her family's poverty and most of the people in her life not taking mental health seriously meant that she never had access to any support. Knowing that she would not survive all four years of high school, she graduated at 16 years old and moved across the country to Los Angeles, California to pursue her passion—a career in performance. Today, Brianna advocates for the people like her who struggle with suicidal thoughts and are not afforded the access to mental healthcare that they so desperately need. She works to enable everyday people to better support someone who is suicidal when they need it. Since finally being able to attend therapy, Brianna hopes to heal and live a happy life.

www.ingramcontent.com/pod-product-compliance
Lightning Source LLC
Chambersburg PA
CBHW060344130626
46553CB00003B/1099